What
Had
Happened
Was…

# What
# Had
# Happened
# Was …

A "Realistic" Way To View A Deal Of A Lifetime

Clyde Anderson

ParaMind Publications
Atlanta, Georgia

ParaMind Publications, LLC
2090 Baker Road Suite 304-171
Kennesaw, Georgia 30144

Library of Congress Catalog Card Control Number: 2004098467

ISBN 0-9762738-0-2

Printed in the United States of America

Contributions by: Jannifer Anderson

Edited by: Juanita Gist

For more information about
What Had Happened Was...
678-574-8376
www.paramindpublications.com

Cover Photography
Copyright © 1997
by Morris Press

Printed in the United States by Morris Publishing
3212 East Highway 30
Kearney, NE  68847
1-800-650-7888

Dedicated to all my clients who have inspired me through their trials and triumphs with credit, I truly thank you. It is because of your stories and courage I'm able to open my heart, listen and understand how to help others. God bless everyone who reads this book. May the understanding of credit you develop help sharpen your sword.

Proverb 27:17 Iron sharpens iron, so one man sharpens another
(New International Version)

To all my friends

Credit (kred'it) n. Trust in ones ability to meet payments when due.

What
Had
Happened
Was…

# Chapter One

## The Special Deal

But the man who looks intently into the perfect law that gives freedom, and continues to do this, not forgetting what he has heard, but doing it-he will be blessed in what he does.
James 1:25 (NIV)

Somewhere between perfect bliss and rock bottom is a place called Reality. Life in Reality is like a fast paced foot race; similar to the world we live in. It can be unkind to those who are not prepared. It can be generous to those who can navigate the avenues well. It's where the strong survive and the weak get left behind, eaten alive, or left out.

Citizens who live in Reality are everyday people who are just trying to make it. Like you and me, they deal with real life situations and their ups & downs. But more importantly, they deal with credit.

The dawn of a new day brought exciting news to Reality. As the good citizens awoke from last nights slumber and ventured out to their various destinations, shiny gold signs with bold green letters met their eyes. A closer look revealed many eyes filled with desire. The signs were everywhere and they read:

**Get Ready
The Special Deal Is
Coming!**

**It's the deal of a
lifetime, what you've
been waiting for, the
answers to all your
questions.  Freedom,
the ability to live out
your dreams!**

It had been a long time since anything this good had happened in Reality. The news was spreading everywhere. It appeared on all the television stations. It was splashed on billboards. It piped from every radio station. Life in Reality was turning inside out. The people of Reality talked about it all over town. They could not believe it. The citizens of Reality could not wait to take advantage of the Special Deal.

One of the first citizens to notice the Special Deal was Tugood Tubetru. He had seen a sign posted on his tree in the front yard as he paced down the driveway to retrieve his daily Economic Street Journal.

"Well what is this all about," Tugood Tubetru said curiously as he stared at the bright gold sign with bold green letters. "That sounds like something I would be interested in."

Tugood Tubetru was never one to miss an opportunity. He then grabbed the paper and headed towards the kitchen to finish his morning coffee before he drove to work.

As Tugood glanced over the headlines in the Economic Street Journal he noticed a big section featuring the Special Deal. The advertisement in the paper looked just like the sign posted in his front yard.

"My goodness, what a deal, what a deal," thought Tugood Tubetru. "How could anyone pass this offer up," he continued.

Tugood thought about how wonderful it would be to have freedom to live out his dreams. He noticed the small disclaimer that stated what the requirements were to receive the Special Deal.

"Possess a strong credit profile and pay your bills on time," Tugood Tubetru said as he read closely. "Why that's easy for me.   This is the best opportunity yet," he said cheerfully. "I'm going to start right away."

Intrigued by the Special Deal, Tugood Tubetru began to prepare diligently.  One of the requirements was to possess a strong credit profile. Tugood knew he had excellent credit. Thus, this first requirement was nothing to worry about. Tugood knew he could verify this with a copy of his credit report.

So, Tugood Tubetru ordered a copy of his credit report, which he did twice a year to see what was being reported.  He also knew that if there were any concerns, he could easily fix them by addressing them early.

Tugood Tubetru was very excited about the deal and wanted to find out more.  He decided to be proactive and contact the Special Deal Headquarters.  The Special Deal Headquarters processed credit profile information, stored credit history data and made all decisions regarding the deal.

Tugood dialed the phone number given in the paper for the Special Deal Headquarters and a representative chimed, "Good Morning Special Deal Headquarters, how can I direct your call?"

"Yes, good morning," replied Tugood Tubetru. "I would like to inquire about the Special Deal I've seen advertised in my neighborhood?"

"Great," replied the representative.
"First let me have your name and personal identification number so we can access your credit report. From there we will see what your requirements are," the representative continued.

"That sounds like a good plan," said Tugood Tubetru.

Tugood cheerfully gave the representative his name and personal identification number. The personal identification number also serves as the key to his personal credit history. The representative put Tugood Tubetru on hold while his information was being processed.

After a brief pause, the representative returned to say, "Tugood Tubetru your credit report looks flawless. Your report shows that you have a history of paying your bills on time, so you are pre-approved for the Special Deal. Your only requirements to receive the Special Deal are to continue paying your bills on time and maintain your flawless credit report."

"Thank you so much, I appreciate your prompt response," Tugood Tubetru modestly replied. Yet inwardly, he was grinning gleefully.

As Tugood Tubetru hung up the phone with the Special Deal representative, he heard a Disk Jockey from one of the local radio stations. The guy said some good citizens in Reality would not qualify for the Special Deal because of poor credit decisions.

But that was not the case with Tugood Tubetru. You see in Reality, Tugood Tubetru was considered special because his personal situation was not like the other citizens. He was considered the one to call on whenever good credit was required.

Tugood remembered being taught as a teenager that paying bills on time is one of the keys to having good credit. He learned that certain bad decisions could have a lasting effect on his credit report, preventing him from purchasing a home, car or even obtaining a credit card.

Tugood was grateful that when he was 18 years old, his parents had made him an authorized user on their accounts. This step had enabled him to establish a good credit report. Since that time, Tugood has remained faithful to his parents' advice. He continues to sustain a positive credit future.

## Authorized User
### Ride someone's back

Do you know someone with good credit?  Ask to be added as an authorized us er on a credit card.  This will build your credit rating as long as the cardholder pays on time. This method of rebuilding works even if you don't have an actual card or never use the account.

# Chapter Two

...But hope that is seen is no hope at all. Who hopes for what he already has? But if we hope for what we do not yet have, we wait for it patiently.
Romans 8:24-25 (NIV)

Several weeks later, Couden Careless sat on the sofa, sulking and feeling sorry for himself. He had just lost another minimum wage job and his mind entertained the thought of filing bankruptcy. Couden Careless could not get from under the debt he had accumulated over the years.

"This is impossible. How am I suppose to make any money when I can't even keep a job", he said hopelessly.

"I got folks calling me everyday about this bill, that bill...I give up."

He was fed up with his circumstances. But he couldn't figure out how to change his life or his debt situation. Then he remembered the Special Deal was coming.

"Who needs a job anyway when you can have freedom," Couden Careless thought. "All my problems will be solved as soon as I get my hands on that Special Deal and freedom."

Meanwhile, Couden Careless searched around for a pen and paper to write down his game plan when he saw a gold and green envelope from the Special Deal Headquarters.

"How did this get here?" he wondered.

"It must have been here for a couple of days because I haven't checked the mail lately," he continued.

When you have as many collection letters as Couden Careless had received, it's easy to avoid the mail.

## Collections
**Bill collectors at your door?**

A bill that goes unpaid will be written or charged off by the company and/or sold to an outside company for collection. However either way, you still owe the money due.

He gazed at the envelope and rubbed his fingers across the gold embossing. He then ripped open the envelope and began to read the card inside:

Get Ready, The Special Deal is Coming!
It's the deal of a lifetime, what you've been waiting for, the answers to all your questions. Freedom, the ability to live out your dreams!

Couden Careless stared in disbelief.

"This is just what I was waiting for...a chance of a lifetime!" he shouted excitedly.

What he failed to realize, was that he first needed to qualify. Qualify- meaning he had to meet the minimum standards set by the Special Deal Headquarters. But when a credit report looks as horrible as his, you have to wonder why Couden Careless thought he would qualify in the first place.

You see, Couden Careless was never educated about credit. He was never taught how certain bad decisions could have a lasting effect on his credit report. Unknowing, he started his own downward spiral. Tragically, he was a victim waiting to happen when he received his first credit card. With that credit card, came another and another. It was great!

He used the tiny pieces of plastic and bought things when he didn't have money…genius!  Then the bills started pouring in and it was hard to juggle all the payments. Especially when Couden Careless was in between jobs.

He got so deep into debt that he simply let his situation go. Couden Careless didn't care anymore and he slipped into a credit coma.  He stopped paying his bills, bounced checks and created collections trailing miles behind.

As a result of his negligent actions, his credit suffered horribly and caused his report to appear derogatory to anyone who viewed it, including employers.

Now Couden Careless checked out the Special Deal. After reading further, he saw the letter.  It read:

SDHeadquarters

N. Limbo Lane
Reality, USA 24683


Dear Mr. Careless,

Due to your derogatory credit history and negligent behavior towards credit, you have the opportunity to apply for the Special Deal under the second chance program. This program is created for people just like YOU who have no regard for their credit, yet still want the same deal as their peers with better credit. If you really want this deal all you have to do is complete the following tasks:

1. Maintain a job for at least six months.
2. Write a letter explaining what happened and what you have learned from your past mistakes.

These are your requirements. After you have completed these things, your information will then be processed for consideration.

Sincerely,


Special Deal Headquarters

"Whatever," he said sarcastically after reading the letter.

"I know my credit can't be that bad, can it?" he said as he began to question himself.

"Besides I heard about somebody getting the deal with worse credit than me, so I know I should get it," he continued.

In Reality, this was only a myth. Getting the Special Deal was a huge opportunity for Couden Careless. One that would get him out of the juggling business. He could not afford to mess this up. If only he really viewed it that way. All he could think about were all the wonderful things he could have with the Special Deal.

Ironically, he gave not one thought to his failing credit conditions or how to change them altogether. Unfortunately, some citizens of Reality have a lot to learn. Couden Careless was one of them.

# Chapter Three

One man pretends to be rich, yet has nothing; another pretends to be poor,
yet has great wealth.
Proverb 13:7 (NIV)

Time moved on in Reality. And more and more citizens were buzzing about the Special Deal. One citizen in particular did not notice all the commotion and excitement surrounding the Special Deal. This citizen was D. Joneses.

D. Joneses had been quite busy lately improving his property. These improvements were not needed for added value. He had seen some of his neighbors make similar changes to their homes and he could not be outdone.

He was determined to have the best looking home in his neighborhood no matter what the cost. His charge card could handle it, so he thought.

An appearance of wealth is very important to D. Joneses. Sometimes he went through extreme measures to get the right appearance.

One beautiful sunny day, D. Joneses strolled around to his backyard to admire his latest handiwork. He had installed a new super-sized Jacuzzi on his marble patio. While outside, D. Joneses overheard a familiar voice.

"That sounds like my next door neighbor," D. Joneses thought, "What is he squeaking about?"

D. Joneses had never admired his neighbor's "squeaky" voice and didn't really like listening to it. But today, his neighbor was bragging about a Special Deal. Disgusted yet intrigued, D. Joneses continued to listen as he heard his neighbor say:

"Get Ready, The Special Deal is Coming!
It's the deal of a lifetime, what you've been waiting for, the answers to all your questions.
Freedom, the ability to live out your dreams!"

A look of curiosity and excitement appeared on D. Joneses' face as he began to wonder about how he could get the Special Deal. D. Joneses felt he needed to act fast, just in case more citizens of Reality found out about the Special Deal.

Determined to find the Special Deal, D. Joneses rushed into his kitchen, grabbed the keys to his luxury car and sprinted out the front door.

Before he could open his car door, he heard his neighbor calling, "Hey! Hey D. Joneses how are you?"

"Great, just great", D. Joneses replied in a loud voice.

The neighbor approached D. Joneses to ask him about the Special Deal and find out if he had turned in his paperwork. In the back of D. Joneses' mind, he knew he hadn't even received a notice. Now D. Joneses' sole mission was to get the Special Deal. And his neighbor was wasting his time! So he abruptly left the neighbor, and sped down the street in his car.

As D. Joneses sped away, he reached for his phone to find the location of the Special Deal Headquarters.

"I'll get to the bottom of this," he spat angrily. "It's obvious they don't know who I am!"

As he reached for his phone, he noticed a small stack of letters on the floor of the car. He recalled taking the mail out of his briefcase and placing it under his seat as he drove to work yesterday. Blast! He had forgotten about it and had left it in the car.

When D. Joneses stopped at a traffic light, he decided to check the mail for any new credit card offers. He loved getting credit card offers. Then he saw the gold and green envelope addressed from the Special Deal Headquarters.

Oblivious of the green light, and the traffic, D. Joneses gazed at the envelope. The shiny green letters gracing the envelope hypnotized him. Eager to read what was inside, he ripped open the envelope.

He quickly skimmed through the letter. When he came to the fine print, it said something D. Joneses was not prepared for. It read:

SDHeadquarters


2 Keep Up Way
Reality, USA 24680

Dear Mr. Joneses,

Due to your history of over indulgence and abuse of credit, you have the opportunity to apply for the Special Deal under the second chance program. This program is created for citizens just like YOU who use their credit for all the wrong reasons, yet still want more so they can keep up with the latest trends of citizens who can really afford true luxuries in life. If you really want this deal all you have to do is complete the following tasks:

1. Don't make any new purchases that are not necessary.
2. Try to pay off as much debt as possible.
3. Don't establish any more credit.

These are your requirements. After you have completed these things, your information will then be processed for consideration.

Sincerely,


Special Deal Headquarters

"This can't be right," D. Joneses said disconcertedly. "I've got to pull over."

Stunned by the idea of having to perform certain tasks in order to receive something he believed he was entitled too, caused D. Joneses to question the validity of the offer. After all maxing out his credit cards was his choice and no one else's.

He felt no one should have the right to question his credit worthiness. He began to wonder which one of his neighbors knew about the deal.

"I've gotten other deals before so this deal should not be a problem," he said without much conviction.

"Besides, if my credit is so bad, why do I keep receiving offers for more?"

You see D. Joneses didn't realize it, but he had a serious problem. He loved material things. He loved credit cards! And he loved being the talk of the town, which he usually was.

With one of the most beautiful homes in the neighborhood, a new top of the line luxury car, a great corporate job and good income, how could you not notice D. Joneses?

He thought his life was great, only there was just one problem…he was nearly broke.

D. Joneses had not given his lifestyle serious thought. Had he thought about his situation, he would have realized that he spends the majority of what he earns on his wonderful lifestyle. When his sizeable monthly income was gone, he used credit cards to take up the slack. As a result of his lavish existence, his credit went from positive to marginal. Too much credit was his issue. D. Joneses' credit was stressed out and maxed out.

The debt that D. Joneses had accumulated, exceeded his monthly income and caused problems each month. D. Joneses sometimes had difficulty paying all his bills by the due date. Unfortunately, that was the price citizen D. paid for living outside his means.

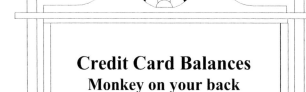

**Credit Card Balances**
**Monkey on your back**

**When a credit balance equals
more than 30% of the credit
limit, it begins to immediately
affect your credit report
negatively.**

**Example: $1000 limit, keep
below $300**

Meanwhile, D. Joneses thought about his requirements for the Special Deal and decided to follow through.

"If I have to change my life for a few months to receive something that will let me live out my dreams forever, I will do it," D. Joneses said.

"This is going to be tough, but not as tough as it could be if my neighbor received this deal and I don't," he thought.

Charged with a mission, D. Joneses steered his car towards home to begin work on his tasks.

As he drove home, D. Joneses daydreamed about all the wonderful things he would buy when he got the Special Deal.

# Chapter Four

We do not want you to become lazy, but imitate those who through faith and patience inherit what has been promised.
Hebrew 6:12 (NIV)

Later that same day, Jestu Getby had just completed his fourth personal call at work. At the same time he decided not to answer any more incoming calls. He wanted to daydream about the life he would live as soon as he figured out how to quit his dead end job.

He often did this after answering about twenty service calls, the minimum required to make his daily quota.

You see Jestu Getby never saw a need to do more than what's required when performing a task.

He firmly believes in doing just enough to get by. He often complains about his job but in a sense he enjoys it. His job allows him to nurture his mentality to perform minimal tasks and pays him enough to survive.

Jestu Getby has perks too. He takes extra long lunches and gets other co-workers to clock out for him when he wants to go home early. This was his way of life. Do just enough to get by.

Meanwhile at work, Jestu Getby was about to make another personal call when an instant message popped up on his computer screen.  It read:

Get Ready, The Special Deal is Coming!
It's the deal of a lifetime, what you've been
waiting for, the answers to all your questions.
Freedom, the ability to live out your dreams!

"What in the world," Jestu Getby murmured as he looked at the screen.  He then looked over both shoulders to see if there were any suspicious looking co-workers lurking around making jokes.

Musing thoughtfully he remembered hearing about a Special Deal on the radio a few weeks ago. Jestu Getby clicked the okay button to accept the offer, now showing on the screen, but nothing happened.  Then slowly a small disclaimer appeared in the middle of the screen.  It stated:

SDHeadquarters

22 Minimal Drive
Reality, USA 24682

Dear Mr. Getby,

Due to your marginal credit report, history of late payments and procrastination, you have the opportunity to apply for the Special Deal under the second chance program. This program is created for citizens just like YOU who want a lot out of life but never want to put any effort into doing anything about it, yet still daydream about a better life, which requires hard work and dedication. If you really want this deal, all you have to do is complete the following tasks:

1.    Pay all bills on time.
2.    Save some money.
3.    Develop a plan to improve your life and set some goals.

These are your requirements. After you have completed these things, your information will then be processed for consideration.

Sincerely,


Special Deal Headquarters

"So this is the deal everyone is crazy about," he said after reading the message.

"I don't know why anyone would go crazy over doing work just to get a deal…that's not special," he murmured.

Jestu Getby could not understand why anyone would want to work to receive something they couldn't have now.

His logic led him to believe that some citizens in Reality receive things that appear to be special all the time by doing the same amount of work, or even less. He couldn't possibly fathom the thought of doing anything extra to get something special in return.

Jestu Getby read the disclaimer again and said, "I don't see how completing those tasks will benefit me anyway. My credit isn't the best, but it's alright."

"I can live with that," he continued.

Jestu Getby did not understand that following through with his requirements was an opportunity to help his marginal credit, and improve his late payment history.

You see, Jestu Getby had a problem breaking old habits of making bad decisions involving credit. He was never educated on credit and how certain bad decisions could have a lasting effect on his credit report.

So naturally he did not understand that procrastinating, paying bills late and missing payment arrangements would cause his credit standing with creditors, including utility companies, to become negative. And his utility services were often subject to disconnection as well.

Jestu Getby's lack of responsibility caused him to live moment-to-moment and unprepared for the future. If events outside the norm happened and he missed a paycheck, Jestu Getby would have difficulty living at his current modest level.

While at work, Jestu Getby considered performing his requirements to get the Special Deal or letting the Special Deal go. He reached a decision.

"Okay, I'll go for it," he said confidently. "The requirements don't seem that bad, but the second I feel like I'm doing more work than I have to, I'll quit."

"Maybe I'll get lucky and change my life," he mumbled.

**Payment Arrangements**
Let's make a deal

If you can't make a payment, contact the company to let them know. Offer a reasonable alternative arrangement that will allow you to make partial payments on specified dates or pay at a later date.

# Chapter Five

## The Special Deal Is Almost Here!
## How They Handle Commitment

A fool gives vent to his anger, but a wise man keeps himself under control.
Proverb 29:11 (NIV)

Over six months have passed and just about every citizen in Reality knew about the Special Deal. The citizens of Reality, who knew about it, still desired the deal, and counted down the months remaining to sign up. Every citizen that is, except Couden Careless.

While relaxing at a friend's house Couden Careless noticed a commercial flash across the television screen.

Have you signed up for your Special Deal?
Time is running out!
Don't miss out on a chance to live out your dreams!

"Oh, no! I forgot about the Special Deal," said Couden Careless.

He jumped up and immediately began thinking about where his offer letter could be. He had opened the letter some months ago. And now he had no idea of where it could be.

Couden Careless had moved in with a friend since his options were minimal. There was a chance the letter could have been thrown away during the move by mistake.

Distraught by the thought that he might have lost the only opportunity he had to change his life, Couden Careless scrambled to find his offer letter. He searched everywhere he believed he could have placed it. Was it in a junk drawer where he usually kept important documents? Or maybe he had thrown it away thinking he didn't need it?

As he rummaged through one of his old gym bags, he found something balled up with juice stains on it.

"I hope this isn't it, looking like this," he said nervously. Unsure of what he discovered, he carefully opened the purple spotted ball and saw it was his offer letter after all.

"I don't know how this ended up in the bag," he thought. "I haven't used this bag in months."

Couden Careless read the offer again to refresh his memory.

Get Ready, The Special Deal is Coming!
It's the deal of a lifetime, what you've been
waiting for, the answers to all your questions.
Freedom, the ability to live out your dreams!

Couden Careless read the letter. He briefly thought about all the time he had wasted between the first time he had read the letter and now. He always shrugged off his tasks and his commitment to accomplish them. Now Couden Careless wanted to kick himself for his usual casual carelessness.

Convinced he had nothing left to lose or do the rest of the day, Couden Careless decided to try and work on his tasks, if it wasn't too late.

He still had not secured a job as required by the offer. He had no choice but to work on his explanation letter. It had been a long time since Couden Careless had to construct such a document, let alone a compelling explanation letter.

After creating several drafts he decided his efforts were good enough and settled on a final draft. His finished letter said:

To Whom It May Concern:

I'm writing this letter because I was told I have bad credit and needed to explain why so I can have a Special Deal.

First of all, I don't owe anything on the car because I gave it back. After I bought it, I realized I could not afford it so I drove it back and left it on the lot with the other cars. I called and left a message that I was giving the car back, but no one ever called me back. If they didn't care about the car, why should I care?

Second, those medical bills are mine but I had insurance so I don't know why they went into collections. I may have paid some bills late but not the credit cards. I thought the credit cards were paid on time. I did live in that apartment but I moved, so I don't know how I could owe any money. Even though I didn't give a notice, I had to move out right away. Yes, I did have a student loan but when I dropped out of school they didn't call me so I didn't call them.

No, I haven't contacted any of my creditors because someone told me all my collections would fall off in seven years anyway. I don't have any information to prove my story but I am telling the truth.

Yours truly,

Couden Careless

## Voluntary Repossession
### Repo's ugly twin

Just because you turn in a  car
or give it back to the dealer
when you can't make the
payments doesn't mean
you're free from the de bt.
This is considered a
voluntary repossession and it
reports negatively on your
credit report the same way it
would if the finance  company
took the car.

With one task completed, all Couden Careless had to do now was secure a job quickly. He currently didn't have one. So he decided to make up a story about being laid off unexpectedly and was desperately looking for a job.

"Surely the Special Deal Headquarters will believe that one," he thought. "That kind of thing happens all the time."

Couden Careless felt a sense of accomplishment. He was actually proud of himself for creating, what he considered to be, a sensible letter as well as a plausible unemployment story. Just as Couden Careless was about to mail his explanation letter he noticed the deadline. It was too late for him to apply! His deadline had expired!

"How could I have missed the deadline to apply?" he groaned.

Frustrated and confused Couden Careless tossed the offer and his explanation letter up in the air. Now angry and confused he needed to take his frustrations out on someone. He called the Special Deal Headquarters to give them a piece of his mind. He felt as though the Special Deal Headquarters had set him up to fail.

Couden Careless grabbed the phone. As he dialed the number and waited for someone to answer, he started thinking about his life before the Special Deal.

"My life was okay until this deal had me jumping through hoops," he said coldly.

But until now, he had not done any work to get the Special Deal.

When the customer service representative answered the phone, Couden Careless screamed, "I have been misled about this Special Deal. I thought I had twelve months to apply."

"I was about to mail in my information when I saw the expiration date in small print," he continued.

"Now I missed the deadline because the print was too small for me to read. What are you going to do about it?" he demanded.

The silence on the other end made Couden Careless even angrier. He continued to rant on and on about how he didn't understand why his past mattered so much anyway. As he further justified his past mistakes, the customer service representative asked him to hold. The representative transferred his call to the second chance department so he could vent there.

After holding for 10 solid minutes, he heard another voice on the other end of the phone. However, this representative had an attitude just like Couden Careless and was not in the mood for his.

She said, "Please be quiet and listen to what I have to say. I've heard your situation before and I am not moved."

"I've spoken to one hundred people today alone. They all had some sort of excuse as to why they missed the deadline to apply, or why they had certain credit issues that prevented them from getting the deal at all," she continued.

It was hard for the representative to listen to the same stories over and over especially without evidence to back them up.

The representative had expected Couden Careless to call anyway. The Special Deal Headquarters was about to send him a letter explaining how he had lost the deal because he missed the deadline.

The representative continued, "You should have been more responsible with your credit in the past, in order to get a Special Deal in the future. Only people who have taken the time to establish and maintain good credit would have no problem getting a Special Deal. If you mess up, the terms of how you may receive future opportunities will be a lot harder."

A blank stare appeared across Couden Careless' face as the representative concluded her lecture.

"You should have known to be aware of some of the pitfalls you fell into.  If only you were educated about credit.  Maybe your situation would have been a lot better," the representative said.

This information made Couden Careless intense.

"How dare she tell me I am uneducated?" he said.

Couden Careless wanted to let the representative have it when she said something that made him pause.  She told him he could still qualify for the deal under a special "change your life or else" clause.

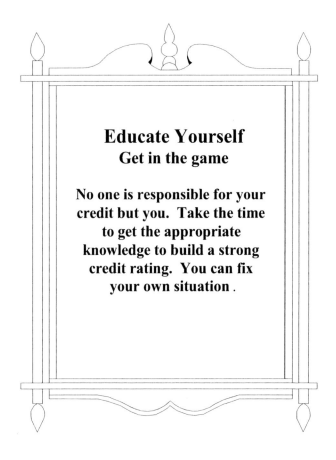

**Educate Yourself**
**Get in the game**

**No one is responsible for your credit but you. Take the time to get the appropriate knowledge to build a strong credit rating. You can fix your own situation .**

The representative started to feel bad that Couden Careless was never taught about credit. She didn't have the ability to go back in time to help him avoid his mistakes. But she could help him find solutions to his errors and possibly start over again.

The problem was, she'd seen so many like him repeat the same mistakes over and over. This caused her not to believe every story she heard. Overtime, she had developed a soft spot. She managed to give certain callers another chance to prove themselves.

Meanwhile, the representative explained to Couden Careless the conditions of the new offer. The tasks were to attend a credit education class, write a report on what he learned, and secure a new job. When the tasks were completed, the Special Deal could possibly be his.

Couden Careless concluded his conversation with the representative and thought to himself how proud he was at handling the situation as he did. He thought that he gave the headquarters a piece of his mind and still got to qualify for the Special Deal. Wait! He didn't know where to go for his class.

Until the headquarters sent him a new letter with all the new details, Couden Careless just sat back comfortably and waited to get started on his new tasks.

# Chapter Six

You do not delight in sacrifice, or I will bring it...the sacrifices of God are a
broken spirit...
Psalm 51:16-17 (NIV)

Across town sitting in the far corner of his bedroom, shaking, sweating and tightly gripping his credit card was D. Joneses. It had been over six months since he had used a credit card. He hadn't made any new purchases except for food, gas and bare necessities.

Committing to the three tasks to get his Special Deal was driving D. Joneses crazy. He cringed every time he noticed his neighbors with new tools, toys and trendy new clothes. He felt as though his clothes and material possessions were old and tattered even though he had purchased some of those treasures only six months ago.

You see D. Joneses was a victim of the "Christmas Scenario."

Remember how you wanted certain toys for Christmas so badly that you thought about them every month? The big day finally arrived and you received your gifts and it was a matter of time before that new feeling wore off.

This was how D. Joneses felt about everything he wanted and purchased. He never understood the concept of delayed gratification.

D. Joneses had put a tremendous effort into not spending frivolously. So much so, he couldn't concentrate on paying off his debt as required for the Special Deal. Besides, D. Joneses felt that since he wasn't spending, there wasn't any debt to repay.

He didn't think about the debt he had racked up months before, bills that he still owed. For D. Joneses, that was in the past. The only thing that kept him going was that in a few months, the Special Deal could be his and his life would be changed forever.

All of his sweating and trembling was going to pay off if he could keep his commitments. But it was hard for him to stay focused on completing his tasks.

Sometimes D. Joneses would get so delirious from spending withdrawals that he would make price tags to put on his old cloths so he could pretend they were new and buy them all over again.

But no matter how delirious he would get, nothing was going to prevent him from getting the Special Deal, especially since his neighbor had found out about it before he had.

## At Least Pay The Minimum Due
### Shame on you

Don't always feel  as
though you have to pay
large sums of money
toward credit card
balances, even though
this helps.  Paying the
minimum due on time
avoids late  payments
from being reported.

Just as D. Joneses was restoring his faith towards his commitments, he turned on the television only to find the Network Vending Channel. There was an exclusive collection available for five minutes to its preferred platinum customers.

"I'm a preferred platinum customer. This collection was designed with me in mind," he said slyly.

"But I can't take advantage of this offer. If I do I will lose my Special Deal," D. Joneses continued.

After gazing at the collection for a few minutes, he recognized it as the same one he'd seen his neighbor with the previous day.

"I can't let my neighbor or anyone else out do me," he said.

Something deep inside told him he had to have this offer. Suddenly he let out a horrible, loud grunt of frustration. Sometimes D. Joneses couldn't understand himself and why he did the things he did.

You see when D. Joneses wanted something he felt he should always have it. Maybe it was something that stemmed from childhood because his parents couldn't afford to buy a lot of material things, or maybe it was just the opposite.

Maybe his parents bought him everything, and now the cycle continues. Who knows, but D. Joneses needed to make a decision. He had to have this new collection. Then he thought that maybe he could take advantage of the five-minute offer in secret. After all, he had already submitted his application for the Special Deal.

"Surely the Special Deal Headquarters has examined my credit profile by now. So no one would have to know about the purchase until after the Special Deal arrived," he said.

"What a plan, if it works out," he continued.

D. Joneses reached for the phone to call the Network Vending Channel to get his five-minute offer, when the phone rang.

He picked up the phone to answer it and found it was only a recording. Ironically, it was a call from the Special Deal Headquarters. It was a courtesy call to make sure he was feeling okay and following the steps to receive his Special Deal.

D. Joneses could not believe what had just happened. This must have been divine intervention. Immediately he thought about how foolish it would have been to not delay his gratification and risk being the only one in his neighborhood without the Special Deal. How could he risk not getting the deal for a few minutes of temporary pleasure?

With that thought, D. Joneses hung up the phone and decided to play his department store game. Back to putting tags on his old clothes, pretending to buy them all over again. Something had to take his mind off waiting for his Special Deal to arrive.

# Chapter Seven

The deeds of faithless men I hate; he will not cling to me.
Psalm 101:3 (NIV)

Later during the week, Jestu Getby was still working toward his Special Deal. The previous months had been very rough for him. Committing to his three tasks had Jestu Getby going in circles.

First, he was supposed to pay all his bills on time, which he still barely did. He made payment arrangements, but because he was not organized he missed deadlines to keep his arrangements. Jestu Getby managed to keep most of his utilities on with only minimal disconnection.

His second task was to save some money, which he struggled to do. How was he supposed to save money when he had to pay all his bills on time? Jestu Getby made a decent living. After he paid all of his bills first, there was barely enough money left over for him to go out and have some fun or buy something new. Saving money was just not realistic.

His third task was to develop a life plan and set some goals. This happened to be the last thing on his mind.

## Set a Budget
### Don't live check to check

**Save money by paying yourself FIRST. It sounds crazy because bill collectors want their money too, but you are more forgiving of yourself than a bill collector. So take care of yourself first, but you must budget to pay those creditors.**

Jestu Getby thought he had lots of time before the Special Deal would arrive. So he procrastinated and didn't bother to begin his life plan. Actually he only had a few days to finish all his tasks before the deadline.

To make himself feel better about the situation, he kept telling himself that he had a lot of responsibilities on his plate, like paying his bills on time. Setting goals was something that had to wait. Plus, he didn't know what type of goals and plans to develop anyway.

Jestu Getby really wanted to get out from under all his bad debt. But he had already convinced himself that the system was not set up for him to succeed. He felt as though his dead end job already required him to work. He didn't want to work outside of his job.

"This is just too much for me to handle. Maybe the Special Deal is out of my reach after all," he said reluctantly.

Jestu Getby battled the idea of whether or not the Special Deal was right for him. Unfortunately, he did not have any examples to influence him. Nor did he have good models. He did not know a lot of other citizens who had very much financially. Those he knew either never talked about their credit or had marginal credit at best.

He had heard of citizens having so called "good credit" but he had never known any personally. Having "good credit" was just not realistic for Jestu Getby.

Growing up, his parents worked very hard to make sure the roof stayed over their heads, the lights remained on and food was on the table by any means necessary. For the most part, the Getby household lived in survival mode.

Jestu Getby's parents had neither the knowledge nor the time to teach their son about credit. They did not know how certain decisions could affect their credit. They could not teach their son what they did not know. Thus Jestu Getby developed his own mentality about paying bills and managing credit.

Gradually, the pressure began to mount until it became too much for him to bear.

"I can't take it anymore!" Jestu Getby screamed.

"All I want to do is go back to the way things were before the Special Deal," he said.

Life was easier and simpler for him when all he had to do was follow his trusty daily routine. It went like this...get up, go to work, eat, sleep...get up, go to work, eat, sleep...and hope to get to watch a couple of hours of television. Sound exciting? If getting the Special Deal caused him to do extra work, then he would have to pass on the offer. What a way to live!

As Jestu Getby pondered the thought of definitely passing up the Special Deal, another person on the other side of town was about to get a special surprise.

# Chapter Eight

Make it your ambition to lead a quite life, to mind your own business and to work with your hands, just as we told you, so that your daily life may win the respect of outsiders and so that you will not be dependent on anybody.
1 Thessalonians 4:11-12 (NIV)

The following morning Tugood Tubetru organized his day and glanced through the daily mail. He had to be cautious of what he opened and discarded these days. He had discovered an erroneous charge account on his credit report several months ago.

Fortunately for Tugood Tubetru, he kept good records and was able to successfully remove the error. As he looked through the stack of letters he saw the infamous gold envelope with green embossing from the Special Deal Headquarters. Tugood Tubetru eagerly opened the envelope and began to read the letter. It said:

SDHeadquarters

1 Perfect Circle
Reality, USA 24681

Dear Tugood Tubetru,

Congratulations!  You have been granted the
"Special Deal" due to all of your hard work, dedication and
commitment to preserving and understanding your credit.
For making good decisions and developing a plan, you've
been able to overcome credit and financial obstacles others
would have failed.

We at the headquarters view you as a role model for
the credit challenged.  Thank you for being a responsible
citizen and taking ownership for your credit and credit
actions.  You have paid your bills as agreed and as a result,
have a wonderful credit rating that can open so many doors
for you- more than money can buy.

As an added bonus, your Special Deal will be
arriving early.  When your Special Deal arrives in a few
days, please enjoy and use it responsibly, which we know
you will.

Sincerely,


Special Deal Chairperson

Tugood Tubetru was ecstatic! "I can't believe this is happening. I am grateful for this opportunity and will use it wisely and responsibly," he vowed.

All of his hard work was paying off. And it definitely takes wise choices and good decisions to maintain a good credit profile. It takes constant vigilance.

Like anything else worth achieving, the more you do it, the easier it becomes. This time Tugood Tubetru was rewarded with the Special Deal...freedom, the ability to live out his dreams.

But you see, in Reality Tugood Tubetru was already receiving the rewards of a good credit rating. He received extended lines of credit with ease, great interest rates on his home and car loans as well as other financial perks. His good credit was serving him well.

Tugood Tubetru maintained a profile creditors love to see. A profile they will always take a chance on because it shows he knows how to manage his bills, his credit, and his life. Getting the Special Deal was the pinnacle, especially since Tugood Tubetru hadn't expected to get the deal so soon.

Now he could go back to his normal routine before the Special Deal arrived which would not be hard to do.

Besides Tugood Tubetru didn't have to change his life, or do anything extra. Thanks to his parents, and his diligence, he had done everything right all along.

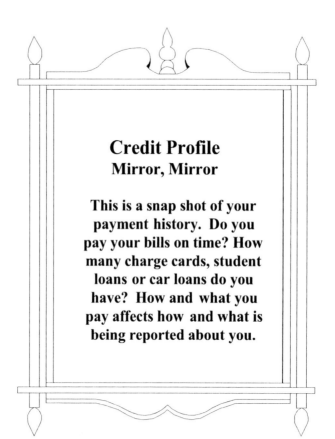

**Credit Profile**
**Mirror, Mirror**

**This is a snap shot of your payment history. Do you pay your bills on time? How many charge cards, student loans or car loans do you have? How and what you pay affects how and what is being reported about you.**

Tugood Tubetru made sacrifices, delayed gratification, budgeted and listened to what other people told him about making the right decisions when it came to obtaining and maintaining his credit.

In Reality, being responsible is what separates the winners from the losers and sometimes the winners can seem too good to be true.

# Chapter Nine

## The Time Has Come
## How They Handle Their Fate

He who scorns instruction will pay for it, but he who respects a command is
rewarded.
Proverb 13:13 (NIV)

There was only a couple of days left. It had been almost a year since the Special Deal first came to Reality. You could still see the bright green and gold signs posted around town.

Everyone was still buzzing with excitement. Others were holding their breath until they learned their fate about the Special Deal. Everyone that is, but Couden Careless.

It was a really stressful time for him right now. He had secured a new job but the credit class he was supposed to take started today. Couden Careless knew the Special Deal was coming very soon but he needed more time to complete his tasks.

Without the Special Deal, Couden Careless could not see himself getting out from under the weight of debt looming over his head. He felt as though the gray clouds always followed him. He didn't understand that his decisions, whether negative or positive, affected his life and dictated its direction.

With only 20 minutes to get to class, Couden Careless rushed out the door and began the long journey to the other side of town. When he arrived at the Credit Education Institute, there was a multitude of people from different ethnic and age groups as well as social classes.

He was very surprised to see so many people with credit hardships just like him. See, Couden Careless thought only certain types of people had credit issues. In Reality there are doctors, entertainers, athletes, business owners, lawyers, and many others who have experienced credit problems as well.

As the class began, Couden Careless' mind started to wonder just the way it did when he was in college. The instructor proceeded to lecture about credit and how it impacts your life. The information was invaluable but fell on deaf ears. Couden Careless heard the instructor speaking but the words didn't seem to stick.

Every time the instructor spoke about a credit pitfall, Couden Careless mentally wandered back to times when he made those same mistakes. Thinking back on how he managed to accumulate so many bad debts gave Couden Careless a sick feeling. But what could he do? The debt was there, the collections were on his report and now he felt that the only way to start over was to come into a great deal of money.

Couden Careless was so consumed with his thoughts that he failed to see he was already in the right place to start over...at the Credit Education Institute. Without proper education and knowledge of how credit works, he could never begin to rebuild, and he would make the same mistakes over and over again.

Meanwhile, a couple of hours went by, which seemed to be an eternity for Couden Careless. And the class was wrapping up. As he looked around the room at everyone's faces, he saw that each person seemed to have a look of fulfillment in their eyes.

Couden Careless watched as everyone else laughed and discussed with one another the key points they had learned in the class. They laughed about their situations now because they understood where the mistakes were made and how to correct them.

He heard people use adjectives like empowered, strengthened and sharpened when referring to how they now felt after attending the class. Couden Careless could not think of a single word that fit how he felt.

Although the speaker had delivered some remarkable information to his audience, Couden Careless missed the message. He was too busy wallowing in his negative credit situation to open his mind to ways of improving it. Before dismissing the class for the five minute break, the instructor announced that there would be a short exam.

"Exam, what exam?" he thought.

Couden Careless had not known about an exam. Tests and exams were always his downfall in school. He rarely tested well.

One of the members saw the frantic nervousness in Couden Careless' face and leaned over and said, "Relax a little, this test is simple! But it is required to get the certificate of completion at the end of the class."

"If you listened to the lecture, the test should be a breeze," the class member continued. "It's just a recap of the information taught during the class."

That was easy for the class member to say. Couden Careless had barely heard a word the instructor said. This was beginning to make him very upset.

Couden Careless began to think that the Special Deal Headquarters had set him up to fail again. When he had spoken to the representative a few months ago, she never said anything about completing an exam.

If Couden Careless had known that, he would not have attended the class. Determined to show the Special Deal Headquarters he was capable of taking the exam, he quickly began to review the handout he received during the class.

"I can take this exam. Besides I've heard people speak about credit before. Fix your credit blah, blah, blah, how hard could it actually be," he said sarcastically.

When the break was over and it was time to take the exam Couden Careless became even more nervous. Couden Careless looked over the questions but did not understand a single one.

Couden Careless thought the answers would be easy. He did not realize that there is no quick fix to understanding and dealing with negative credit.

The best way to understand and move forward is to be educated on how to approach, handle and repair a negative situation and turn it into a positive one.

Angry and confused about what to do next, Couden Careless finished his exam. He did the best he could and walked out of the classroom into an uncertain future.

Doubt consumed him as he said, "I guess I'll go home and not go to work. I probably failed the test. And I've probably ruined my chances of getting the Special Deal again."

While Couden Careless relaxed at home, which doubled as his mother's basement, he heard his mother yell down the stairs for him to pick up the telephone. The Special Deal Headquarters was waiting to speak with him.

Before Couden Careless could even say hello the representative said, "We are very disappointed to hear about your failure."

At that moment, Couden Careless realized he had definitely failed the exam.

The representative continued to say, "Although you were granted a second, as well as a third chance to receive the Special Deal, you still fell short of the minimum requirements needed to receive it. The Special Deal Committee has decided that you can not and will not qualify for the Special Deal unless you change your life, views and attitude towards credit."

Couden Careless was speechless. A look of disbelief appeared on his face, along with a feeling of anger. He was appalled that the Special Deal Headquarters would call him at his mother's house and disrespect him in such a manner.

"How dare the representative tell me I need to change my life?" he thought.

Couden Careless felt he had changed his life several months ago when he tried to perform all those tasks to get the Special Deal. Now he couldn't have it.

He felt his tongue getting loose. He was ready to tell the representative just what to do with the Special Deal. Suddenly he heard a loud click and then the dial tone. Couden Careless could not believe the representative had hung up the phone and disregarded what he was about say.

Crazed with anger, he tried to return the call to give the headquarters a piece of his mind. But when he tried to call back, the operator said the number was no longer valid and to check the number again. Couden Careless could not believe what he was hearing.

"Someone just called me less than five minutes ago," he said.

"Oh who cares anyway?" he thought to himself.

He's right, who cares anyway? If you do not take the time to nurture your credit, then who will?

You must seize the opportunities as they are presented to you to make your life better.

Couden Careless was presented with chance after chance to improve his credit profile. Unfortunately, he was unwilling to take the necessary steps to change his attitude or his views towards credit, all of which would have led to an improved lifestyle. And like his name says, he couldn't care less about it one way or the other.

## Take Responsibility
### You can't hide

It's your credit and no one
else is responsible for your
actions.  Don't just throw
your hands up in defeat.
Things may seem
overwhelming at times but
they are always manageable.
If you make the right
decisions and get the proper
education your credit score
will increase.

# Chapter Ten

People who want to get rich fall into temptation and a trap and unto many
foolish and harmful desires that plunge men  into ruin and destruction.
1 Timothy 6:9 (NIV)

Later that morning D. Joneses leaned beside his mailbox
with his telephone in hand.  He was waiting like he'd been doing
for the past few weeks.  He figured it should be time for the
Special Deal Headquarters to send him his deal in the mail or
give him a call to let him know when it would arrive.

Either way, D. Joneses was determined to get his
Special Deal.  After all this time nothing had changed.  He
had the same mentality before the deal came…give me, give
me, and give me more.

He spent so much time waiting for the deal to arrive.
He didn't eat or sleep and he had stopped caring about his
appearance.  D. Joneses fell into deep despair and looked
like a shell of his former flashy self.

Hours passed and there was no sign of the postmaster. Disappointed yet again, D. Joneses pulled his weak, feeble body from the mailbox and staggered back into his home. Once inside, D. Joneses plunked down on the sofa and watched a little television. He had to take his mind off his disappointment. Suddenly without warning, a message popped up on his "big screen" television. It read:

This Is Your Last Chance!
Get This Great Deal Today! Don't Wait!
The best deal in town until another one just like it comes along. Want to feel good now? Just call now!
Have your credit card ready and BUY NOW!

D. Joneses felt something rise up inside him. At first he thought he was delirious, especially since he wasn't taking care of himself these days. This thing inside him was happiness! He was delirious with joy and happiness! But the message was real! D. Joneses started thinking about this offer and how tempting it was.

He thought, "Why wait for something special when I can have something that sounds great right now?"

Anxious to feel good for the moment, D. Joneses grabbed the phone and called the number displayed on the screen. Before he knew it, he had purchased his very own great deal.

He figured this wouldn't hurt his chances of getting the Special Deal since only one day was left until the official day arrived. Not only that, he would have a great deal and soon the Special Deal! Who could top that?

D. Joneses flooded his mind and imagination with thoughts of all the lavish things he would buy with both of his deals when there was a loud knock at the door. D. Joneses stumbled up from the sofa and staggered to the front door. When he opened the front door he saw a certified letter on the ground.

"This was fast," he thought.

"I wasn't expecting to receive the great deal so soon. I thought it would take at least a day to arrive," he continued.

D. Joneses had forgotten that the Special Deal was to arrive any day now. And today happened to be his day.

He slowly bent down to retrieve the letter, only to find to his surprise that the return address said Special Deal Headquarters. Beads of perspiration started to form on D. Joneses forehead. His hands started to shake nervously as he opened the green and gold envelope.

Anticipating what was inside, he quickly opened the letter. Rather than exciting news, the letter said something that made D. Joneses faint right there on the front porch. It said:

SDHeadquarters

2 Keep Up Way
Reality, USA 24682

Dear Mr. Joneses,

Thank you for applying for the Special Deal. Unfortunately, we are unable to grant you the Special Deal at this time due to your abuse of credit. Several months ago we extended an offer asking you to complete three simple tasks. However, you fell short of fulfilling each one properly. What you have failed to realize is that you obtain and use your credit for the wrong reasons. Stressing your credit in order to buy things you either don't need or can't really afford and purchasing material things to keep up in order to make you feel more important is not the answer. All you are doing is living outside of your means and that, as you know very well can be very stressful. Good luck in the future.

Sincerely,


Special Deal Committee

Reading this letter caused D. Joneses much heartache. Yet it was true.

D. Joneses should have known that living outside of your means and trying to keep up with everyone can be stressful. Especially when you don't really know what or whom you're keeping up with.

Don't waste your credit, because when you need it most, you'll find it won't be there to help you. Be cautious of how you use credit or you will truly find out what happens to those who use it to try and keep up with the Jones's.

# Keep it Real
## Know your limits

Is the weight of the world on
your shoulders?  Don't be
something you are not.   Be
yourself.  Don't go into debt
just to have something because
you think everyone else has it.
Learn to live within your
means.  The look of wealth is
nothing compared to actually
having it.

# Chapter Eleven

For the waywardness of the simple will kill them, and complacency of fools
will destroy them.
Proverb 1:32 (NIV)

Jestu Getby finally learned his fate regarding the Special Deal. He learned the news while at work. As he walked down the hall to his desk, he started grumbling out loud. He knew his co-workers could hear him.

"No one better not bother me or say anything to me today because I had a rough night last night and I don't want to be entertained by someone else's drama," Jestu Getby said. Actually everyone ignored him.

He had almost arrived at his desk when he heard several co-workers bragging about the Special Deal and how wonderful it had been to receive something so great. Everyone was laughing and sharing stories about how the Special Deal was changing their lives.

Jestu Getby had almost forgotten about the Special Deal. It had been several months since he thought about it. Some time ago Jestu Getby had decided that he probably wouldn't be able to get the Special Deal. So he moved on with his life.

Once Jestu Getby arrived at his desk, he quickly logged onto his computer. He wanted to visit the Special Deal website and see what everyone was chattering about. There it was, the sign he'd seen so many times before right on his screen.

Those bold green letters seemed to be hypnotic. The Special Deal is Coming! It's the Deal of a Lifetime… As he read on, he saw stories from people all over the city who had received the deal. He read how the deal had changed their lives. Some lives were changed forever.

One story Jestu Getby read was from a single mother who had worked very hard to establish a better life for herself and her son. This single mother testified about how wonderful the deal was. She said understanding credit, making sacrifices to pay on time and balancing her spending had enabled her to secure the Special Deal.

She concluded her story by writing how she and her son's lives had changed and how they will enjoy the benefits of the Special Deal for years to come.

Moved by the courageous story, Jestu Getby started to think that maybe he had acted a little too hasty. Maybe he should not have abandoned the Special Deal several months earlier. He continued to navigate through the testimonials when he came to another story that interested him.

This story was about a young man who learned early that there is a thin line between credit use and abuse. The young man had destroyed his credit and had not known how to fix it.

Then he had learned about the Special Deal. He felt empowered to educate himself about credit and follow the simple tasks required to improve his credit conditions.

Jestu Getby continued to read as the young man concluded his story. As a result of the hard work put into correcting the young man's credit deficiencies, he was now on the right track to credit recovery and was able to secure the Special Deal.

"These people were all just lucky," said Jestu Getby.

These stories seemed too good to be true, until he stumbled on one that was from a co-worker whose desk was right next to his.

Earlier in the morning when Jestu Getby had first arrived at work, he thought he had heard her boasting about something. He hadn't connected her boasting to the Special Deal. As he read her story he was amazed to see she opened her story by identifying her previous situation. It was just like his!

Jestu Getby's co-worker wasn't educated about credit. She thought like Jestu Getby, that it was too hard to stay on track when you don't make a lot of money. She had realized that it is not how much money you make but how much money you spend that affects your credit.

As Jestu Getby continued reading his co-workers story, he read that after securing her Special Deal she had used it to make much needed improvements in her life.

But, before she had received her deal, she had educated herself about credit and followed the simple tasks required to improve her conditions. Now she was embarking on a new path that allowed her to leave her present job and secure a more fulfilling career. All because she had received the Special Deal.

Jestu Getby finished reading her story with mixed emotions. His feelings were a mixture of jealousy and disappointment.

He was jealous, because someone he knew was actually leaving the dead-end place he had called work for the past several years. He was disappointed, because he realized he could have had similar good things happen to him. If only he had taken the initiative and the time to do those extra tasks to secure his Special Deal. Jestu Getby sat back from the computer. Now sitting at his desk, he was deeply disappointed and saddened.

It bothered him that he had had an opportunity to change his life and move forward but instead had wasted it. Jestu Getby believed things could not get any worse.

Later that day he received an email from the Special Deal Headquarters. Jestu Getby hoped that maybe today would be his lucky day. That there was still a chance for him to receive the deal. Reluctantly he opened the email and braced himself for whatever the message said. It read:

To:        Jestu_Getby@mediocre.com
From:      Special_Deal_Committee@SDH.com
Subject:   Special Deal Status

                          SDHeadquarters

Thank you for applying for the Special Deal. However
due to your procrastination, lack of drive and unwillingness
to make efforts to improve your current situation, we are
unable to grant you the Special Deal.  We don't have
anything else to say to you because we don't feel like
putting forth the effort to write more about your situation.
Good luck in the future.

Sincerely,


Special Deal Committee

Jestu Getby could not believe what he was reading. He felt slighted by the Special Deal Headquarters. He was hoping to have another chance, but in Reality you only get so many chances to change.

The message was true. Jestu Getby missed opportunities to progress and grow primarily because of his poor decisions and lazy actions.

You cannot spend your life just trying to get by, or you will close the door to abundant opportunities.

In order to get something positive out of life, you have to do something positive. The same is true and applies to credit. There is no luck involved in developing and maintaining good credit, just initiative and wise decisions.

## You Have to Do More
### No pain, no gain

**Minimum coverage won't work. Strive to do more than get by. Life has so much to offer. Walking on a tight rope can be dangerous. There are many opportunities for you to FALL OFF!**

# The Day After
# Back to Reality

He who ignores discipline comes to poverty and shame, but whoever heeds
correction is honored.
Proverb 13:18 (NIV)

The Special Deal seemed to have arrived within a blink of an eye. It seemed to have happened so quickly that the citizens of Reality were in a tailspin. The Special Deal caused all citizens to face their credit head on. What these individuals had to learn was that in order to take advantage of special offers, they had to examine their lives and possibly make some changes.

The citizens in Reality either received the deal or did not. It was just that simple.

After twelve months of hype, there were no more glittery signs advertising the deal. No more gold and green envelopes arriving in the mail. No more phone calls to notify anxious citizens. No more messages to alert curious souls.

Some of the citizens without deals had animosity toward the ones with deals. But that was to be expected. After all that's reality.

However, some of those without the deal had vowed never to make the same mistakes again. So that maybe next time, they would be able to enjoy the benefits of a Special Deal.

Then of course there were others who vowed to do nothing because they did not learn from their mistakes. Remember, in Reality that is what separates the winners from the losers.

Tugood Tubetru, D. Joneses, Jestu Getby and Couden Careless all learned their fate regarding the Special Deal. Some did not accept the outcome; nevertheless the decisions were made.

Of the four characters depicted in our story, Tugood Tubetru was the citizen who received the Special Deal. He was the one who understood the benefits of learning about and understanding his credit. He knew how to make his credit work for him- not against him. In Reality it is smart to have "good credit."

Some may think that Tugood Tubetru is just that -too good to be true. However, in our reality, there are dozens of citizens who receive "special deals," but not without hard work.

Tugood Tubetru, D. Joneses, Jestu Getby and Couden Careless reside in all of us to some degree. It's up to you to determine which characteristic will dominate.

Do you want to live your life dodging creditors? Do you want to always have to use cash? Or do you want to have someone else reserve your hotel rooms and rent a car for you?

Do you want to always breath a sigh of relief at the end of each month because you just made it? Are you barely paying your bills with a few late payments along the way? Are you barely able to save for the future?

Do you feel as though you have to use all your earnings to portray a lifestyle that is not realistic? Are you portraying a lifestyle that is nothing more than a facade?

Do you want your life to appear as though everything is great when it really is not? Is your credit card screaming for relief? Is your car payment weighing heavily on your back? Are you consumed with making more to consume more?

Or do you want to be in control of your credit and financial future? Do you want to be prepared for emergencies? They will arise. Do you want to be confident if potential employers check your credit? Do you want to be confident and at ease when your credit is pulled if you make purchases? Can you lean on your credit like a friend when you need to?

How you answer these questions will determine how your story will read.

So in reality, are you waiting for a Special Deal?

### The End

Whatever you do, work at it with all of your heart, as working for the Lord, not for men, since you know that you will receive an inheritance from the Lord as a reward. It is the Lord Christ you are serving.
Colossians 3:23-24 (NIV)

# Answers to Frequently Asked Questions

1.      What is a credit report?

It is a report that contains detailed information about your credit history as it has been reported to the credit reporting agencies by lenders who have extended credit to you. It gives lenders a broad view of your credit history.

2.      How do I obtain a copy of my credit report?

You can get a free copy of all three credit bureaus by going to: www.annualcreditreport.com.

or

Contact all three credit reporting agencies to request:

Equifax #1-800-685-1111
www.equifax.com

Trans Union #1-800-916-8800
www.transunion.com

Experian #1-888-397-3742
www.experian.com

3. How often should I pull my credit report?

You should pull your report at least once per year. Review it thoroughly for accuracy and to catch any errors quickly.

4. What is a good credit score?

Credit Scores can range from 300 to 850, 300 being the lowest. 660 to 720 credit scores are usually considered good, but above 720 is great.

5. How is a credit score determined?

Credit scores are determined by the credit reporting agencies' scoring model that was developed by Fair Isaac & Company. The model takes into consideration information about you and your credit experiences, such as your bill paying history, the number and type of accounts you have, late payments, collection actions, outstanding debt and age of your accounts.

The credit reporting agencies compare this information to the credit performance of other consumers with similar profiles. The scoring system awards points for each piece of information or factor that helps predict who is most likely to repay a debt. The total number of these points is known as a credit score and it helps predict how likely it is that you will repay a loan in a timely manner.

6.     How can I remove false information from my report?

Review your report and tell the credit reporting agencies in writing what information you believe is inaccurate. Include the full company name of the disputed item, the account number and the reason for the dispute.

Send copies of any documents that support your dispute, such as letters from creditors to show accounts were either paid or the information is incorrect.

Identify what you would like deleted or corrected. Then circle those items on the credit report and return the credit report to the credit reporting agencies by certified mail in order to document what the agencies have received.

Keep copies of all your letters and documents. The agencies must investigate the items in question usually within 30 days. Make sure you follow up with them in 30 days to check the status of your claim. If this information can not be verified it must be deleted from your file.

7.     What is the difference between a collection and a charge off?

       There really isn't a difference. A collection is an account
       that was unpaid so the creditor turns it over to its collection
       department to recover the funds or sells it to a third party to
       collect on their behalf.

       The term charge off is used when a company writes off
       this uncollected amount as a bad debt. Contrary to popular
       belief, this does not clear your responsibility.


8.     Is it true that collections and other negative information
       fall off your credit report in 7 years?

       When negative information on your report is accurate,
       only the passage of time can assure its removal. Accurate
       negative information can generally stay on your report for
       7 years from the date of last activity.

       There are certain exceptions; information about criminal
       connections may be reported without a time limitation,
       bankruptcy for 10 years, a lawsuit or unpaid judgment can
       be reported until the statue of limitation runs out.

9.     Should I file bankruptcy if I can't pay all of my bills?

It's really important to analyze your situation and be realistic about what you can handle.

For example, if you owe a small sum of money that could be paid off by setting a budget, bankruptcy may not be the best alternative.  To be certain if bankruptcy is right for you, consult an attorney.  When consulting with an attorney, inquire about the two types of options.  Chapter 7 forgives the bad debt and Chapter 13 is a repayment plan for the debt.  Whichever route is for you, seek a professional and don't try to do it on your own.

10.    What is the difference between installment and revolving debt?

An installment loan is a loan where the amount of the payment is predetermined or fixed, i.e. car payments.

Revolving accounts require at least a specified minimum payment each month plus a service charge on the balance. As the balance declines, the amount of the service charge or interest also declines and vice versa.

11. I voluntarily gave a car I couldn't afford back to the dealer. How will that affect my credit?

A voluntary turn-in is nothing more than repossession by another name. It's just as if the finance company took the car.

The damages for a voluntary repossession affect your report the same as repossession.


12. How many times should I dispute items on my report?

Do not over dispute an item. Disputing items repeatedly sends a red flag to the credit reporting agencies. They become suspicious of your actions and become less likely to investigate whether an item is false or not.

Some repair companies tell you if you dispute the item you want removed over and over they will get tired of researching and remove. This is not accurate, most of the time they view these claims as frivolous.

13. I mailed my credit card payment before the due date and the creditor still reported me late. Can you explain this?

Always communicate with your creditor to make sure you have ample time for a payment to reach their office to avoid late payments when you're sending through the mail. Check into alternate methods of delivery if you are close to the due date.

If you made any late payments in the past, you may have a late fee that if left unpaid will still cause your payment to be late. This is referred to as a Rolling Late.

14. How long do I have after college before my student loans are due?

Most lenders give you a grace period of 6 months after graduation, but you must check with your lender as soon as you know you will be exiting the institution to review the terms of your loan and determine your options.

There are several options available to defer your student loan for several years, which will put your account in a hold status or forbearance. This will allow you to save a lot of time, money and anxiety if you contact them instead of them tracking you down.

Always make sure they have a current address and contact information for you.

15. Is it a good idea to co-sign for a friend's car?

    If you can avoid co-signing for someone, it is the best thing to do. By co-signing you take on half the responsibility to repay the debt. And if the person you co-sign for does not pay, the creditor can make you responsible for the balance and report derogatory information on your credit report as well as any late payments that were made on the account.

16. Someone stole checks out of my home and assumed my identity. How can I prove this on my credit report?

    First contact each of the three major credit reporting agencies. Tell them to include a fraud alert on your credit report, which is a statement that alerts the creditors to get your permission before opening any new accounts in your name.

    Request a copy of your report. Contact the creditors of any accounts that may have been affected, and follow up in writing. File a police report with your local police where the theft took place. Keep copies of all documents in case your creditors need proof of the crime.

17. Is it true that you don't have to pay medical collections if you had medical insurance?

Just because you have medical insurance doesn't always assure you are completely covered. Errors do occur where doctors or hospitals don't receive payments or fees owed from insurance companies. When these payments aren't made regardless of who is really responsible, the delinquency shows up on your credit report, therefore it's your responsibility to correct.

They can usually be resolved easily if you catch it pretty quickly and you can provide documentation that verifies you were covered at the time of service and the insurance company was responsible for that amount.

# Quick Notes

Always pay when due.  Even if it is the minimum.

Set a budget and use as a road map to get to where you want to be.

Watch inquiries-excessive inquiries lower your rating.

Keep important documents on file.  Anything that can later verify proof of payments or closed accounts.  The burden of proof is on you.

Communicate with creditors.  Make payment arrangements where possible.  Creditors just want their money and they appreciate you for being proactive and taking responsibility.  Most times they will work with you.

Always pay late fees.  These can accumulate and cause your accounts to be past due and possibly fall into collections.

Keep balances of credit cards below 30% of the limit.

If you've paid your credit card on time for at least 12 months ask for a credit line increase.

Review the terms of all accounts.

Do not borrow from High Risk finance companies.

Always get letters to show $0 balance when closing accounts.

Negotiate Collections beginning at 30%

# Resources for Your Rights

CRA (Credit Reporting Act): To insure that prospective buyers of the services of credit repair organizations are provided with the information necessary to make an informed decision regarding the purchases of such services and to protect the public from unfair or deceptive advertising and business practices by credit repair organizations.

FCRA (Fair Credit Reporting Act): Designed to promote accuracy and ensure the privacy of the information used in consumer reports.

ECOA (Equal Credit Opportunity Act): Ensures that all consumers are given an equal chance to obtain credit. This doesn't mean all consumers who apply for credit receive it.

FTC (Federal Trade Commission): Which is the Government agency, which works for the consumer to regulate the above acts and prevent fraudulent, deceptive and unfair business practices in the marketplace. It also provides information to help consumers spot, stop and avoid these practices. To file a complaint or get free information on consumer issues, visit www.ftc.gov or call toll free 1-877-653-4261. The FTC insert internet, telemarketing, identity theft and other fraud-related complaints into the Consumer Sentinel, a secure online database available to hundreds of civil and criminal law enforcement agencies in the U.S. and abroad.

# Share It With Others

Order individual copies, quantity discounts for bulk purchases for sales promotions, premiums, fund-raising, or educational use. Special books or book excerpts also can be created to fit specific needs.

Telephone ParaMind Publications at:

678-574-8376

Or write: 2090 Baker Road Suite 304-171 Kennesaw, GA 30144.

For What Had Happened Was… Training Material and All Other Learning Product Information:

www.paramindpublications.com

What Had Happened Was… ISBN 0-9762738-0-2     $10.00 US ($18.00 CAN)

ORDER FORM FOR CONSUMERS ONLY (1-5 Copies)

Payable in US funds only.  Book price: $10.00 each copy. Postage & handling: US $2.75 for one book, $1.00 for each add'l book not to exceed $6.75.

We accept Visa, MC, AMEX ($10.00), and money orders.  No checks or cash/COD.

Call 678-574-8376 or mail your orders to:

ParaMind Publications.                  Bill my
2090 Baker Road Suite 304-171    creditcard _____ exp_____
Kennesaw, GA 30144                        _____Visa_____MC_____AMEX

Signature: _____

Bill To: _____
Address: _____
City: _____ST_____ZIP_____
Daytime phone # _____
Ship To: _____
Address_____
City_____ST_____ZIP_____

Book total................................................................$_____
Applicable sales tax....................................................$_____
Postage & Handling.....................................................$_____
Total amount due........................................................$_____

Please allow 4-6 weeks for US delivery. CAN./Int'l orders please allow 6-8 weeks.
This offer is subject to change without notice.          Ad#